You CAN Do This!

An In-Depth Look at the Digital Marketing Essentials Necessary for Distributors to Remain Competitive and Positioned for the Future

Susan M. Merlo
Jon C. Dupree

ISBN: 1508621012
ISBN-13: 978-1508621010

FOREWORD

As a consultant to wholesale distributors, board member of several trade associations, and a recovering distributor myself, I have a "floor seat" to what's happening – and not happening – at some of the best companies in our business. A thorn in the lion's paw at even some of the distribution industry's top performers is what to do about digital marketing.

My friend and colleague Susan Merlo, who advises companies (including some distributors, and including our firm) about digital marketing, has written a book with her friend, Jon Dupree, that distributor leaders must read.

In case you think "digital" is just a fad or a trend, consider that more and more of your customers and employees were born after 1980. Your digital destiny is that the millennials will be the largest segment by the time most baby boomers retire.

My son just took a job at GrubHub (ticker: GRUB). This mobile and online food ordering company sent over $1 billion of meal orders to over 4 million unique customers in the last 12 months. Yet you may not have heard of them until you saw their ads during the Superbowl. As Matt Maloney, GrubHub's co-founder and CEO says, "Innovation works best when there is a problem to solve".

Invest two hours in your company's future now, and read this book about digital marketing – mobile and online – for your distribution business.

Brent R. Grover
Evergreen Consulting, LLC
Author, *The Little Black Book of Strategic Planning for Distributors*

TABLE OF CONTENTS

INTRODUCTION

Wholesale distribution companies will find themselves at a serious disadvantage if they don't have the correct digital marketing essentials in place. In today's world of instant gratification and instant delivery of information, if you cannot provide the information that your customer needs, or answers to questions that a prospect is asking, expect to find yourself left in the dust. The good news is ... **You CAN Do This!**

In the past, it was the biggest companies with the deepest pockets who were able to attract and retain the best business because they could easily get their advertising into the public eye and outshine the small guys. The big companies had the largest sales teams, bought the biggest ads in the trade journals, and manned the biggest booths at the trade shows.

Today, the playing field is level. The race to the front of the line will NOT be won by the distributors with the most spending power. The race to the front WILL be won by the distributors who are willing to make the effort toward generating valuable content, using the most efficient technology and most of all – listening to what their customers want, and then delivering on the goods.

And by the goods, we mean information. By goods, we mean **a value proposition that leaves a customer or a prospect feeling cared about or listened to, and leaves you and your company positioned as a thought-leader and a leader in your industry.** It's that simple.

The leading distributors will be those who can anticipate what their ideal customers need, sometimes before customers knows it themselves, and give it to them. Whether someone is looking to purchase your product, or would like to learn more about your company, or perhaps they need some industry-specific information that doesn't relate directly to your product or your company, the distributors who understand their customers' problems and needs and can resolve them without being "salesy" will be the distributors who will lead the pack.

So how will you know what brings someone to your website and ensure that visitor's quest is easily met? This can be a stressful challenge for most distributors because you know if a visitor's quest isn't met, they'll find another distributor to meet his or her needs; and with that thought often comes paralyzing pressure. The answer to that question, though, is answered throughout this book, and will become clearer as you read on.

For many distributors, a powerful digital marketing strategy is already a driver of revenue. As more millennials enter the workforce, there's no question that that number of distributors who harness the power of the internet will grow. Over the next five years, it's safe to assume that the choices you make for your company regarding its digital marketing strategy will not only impact your revenue, but also your recruiting efforts, your internal communication efforts, and perhaps even affect your ability to raise financial equity when necessary.

The challenge to meet, therefore, is not just to have a digital marketing strategy in place, but rather to recognize it is a central strategy for your company's success, <u>if</u> the strategy is executed effectively and efficiently. Once your company has decided on a digital marketing strategy, and it has been running a while, it's even more imperative that the company is fully committed to the long-term view. There is nothing more deflating about a company than to see its marketing messages peter out midstream because there wasn't enough support from the top to keep the marketing machine going. It's damaging publicly and internally as well. A company's Facebook page or Twitter feed or blog that hasn't been populated in months is like a forgotten, abandoned ghost town. It gives the impression that the company either 1) had no real commitment, 2) didn't know how to execute, or 3) simply gave up. All three possibilities leave a negative impression of your company.

And while a good digital marketing strategy requires commitment, planning, and most of all, discipline, it isn't difficult to do as long as you have the right players in place. The right players have a willingness to learn the technology, an understanding of the marketing strategies deployed, a good comprehension of the business and its customers, and a commitment to seeing the company succeed.

Depending on your budget, this need could be filled by a handful of willing staff members, or it could be outsourced to an experienced, committed marketing agency. A combination of both would be ideal, and here's why.

No one knows your company better than your employees, especially the employees who have been with you for many years. From those employees will come some of the most valuable information about the company. If you're lucky, you'll have a team that can share the success stories of the past and share openly about the information customers and prospects want, delivering that information in a style that the outside world finds appealing.

You'll also need the expertise of an outside agency to deliver the information; to ensure that when your customers or prospects are looking for information, they find you. After all, if they cannot find you in the search engines, what good is all that information?

Search engines today are smart, and they get smarter every day. They put a premium on fresh, new robust content, considering it most relevant. They use voice recognition technology to deliver videos and podcasts in their results. This emphasis on 'freshness' and relevance means that search engines will quickly deliver the most relevant, robust and precise information first, and old outdated information will be pushed further down the results pages. If a prospect is searching for a product or service you provide, and they're not familiar with your company, finding you will be solely dependent on the content you regularly share online in order to get you noticed before your competitors. In other words, if you're not sharing and properly promoting good content, they won't find you.

The idea of having to navigate the waters of search can be overwhelming at best to the average distributor; just know that there are agencies (like ours) who know the ropes and can help your team navigate the waters.

You may also find comfort in knowing that with technology having evolved to where it is today, marketing results are much more measureable than ever before. Remember the old adage "I know half of the marketing I pay for is working; unfortunately I don't know which half"? Today, marketing and advertising on the internet is so precise, so measureable, so targeted and so effective, that many companies no longer see marketing as an expense, but rather a revenue generator.

Here's a simple example of how that works:

Ace Distributors has a Google ad that, when clicked, brings a visitor to a landing page where the visitor can "opt-in" to receive a special offer from the company. Each time the ad is clicked, it costs Ace $3. So that Google can get paid, of course, they'll let Ace know exactly how many times the ad is clicked, giving them the ability to track what they spend on the ad.

Ace can track, too, how many people come to the page, how long they stay on the page, and whether or not they opt-in to the special offer, which is their goal, harvesting the visitors' contact information.

Let's say for every ten people who land on the page, one visitor opts-in. We know then that for every $30 Ace spends on the Google ad, they get one opt-in. That's $30 per opt-in or lead generated. From there, a lead would be nurtured and eventually handed off to Ace's sales team.

Let's also say that history tells us that for every twenty leads handed off to the sales team, one deal is closed. Therefore, now we know that the average out-of-pocket cost per successful lead for Ace is $600 ($30 x twenty leads = one deal closed).

$600 per successful lead may seem like quite an expense, but when we consider that Ace Distributor's average customer has a lifetime value of $10,000, do you think that, in this case, marketing is an expense or a revenue generator?

Ah, if it were always that easy. In this case, marketing is indeed a revenue generator, but will only remain so as long as the campaign is closely monitored. You may discover that eventually one out of nine people opt-in, or one out of eighteen prospects will become customers, in which case your cost per lead is lower and your revenue is higher.

Or, on the other hand, a competitor may raise their Google marketing budget, forcing you to raise yours. (Google was smart when they designed their Ad Words program; they made it an auction). The cost of that Google click may increase from $3 to $5 or more, in which case it may no longer be profitable to run the ad.

Truth be told, the key to good marketing isn't as simple as running a Google ad – if that were true, more people would do it. The key is creating a buyer experience throughout your marketing funnels that makes a buyer want to be YOUR buyer. Your knowledge, your history, your style and your company's culture are all part of your marketing strategy, and it's a combination of all of the above that will have customers getting to know you better, like you more, and trust you above the rest.

If you were to compete on price alone, well, your customers would be loyal only as long as you maintained the lowest price. Rather, if you were to compete on relationship strength, a strong and loyal bond is what will be most long-lasting through time.

If you're reading this book, chances are you're a wholesale distribution business owner or executive who understands the importance of marketing on the internet today and all we've touched on so far. You understand that traditional marketing methods are less effective and more expensive, and you know that by neglecting to use the internet to market your business, you're missing out on the powerful business results that an effective marketing strategy can give you.

Whether your distribution business is just getting started with digital or online marketing or you're interested in brushing up on the basics, we're glad you're here; we're looking forward to guiding you as you set up and implement a successful internet marketing strategy, and teaching you about the key essentials you'll need to stay ahead of the competition.

We'll take you through an in-depth overview of digital marketing essentials for distribution companies, and you'll learn which marketing essentials will have your company best-positioned as an industry leader, building stronger bonds with your customers and prospects, increasing your sales, and generating substantially more leads. You'll learn, too, that your company can use digital marketing to create new relationships with prospects and turn them into customers, and that digital marketing will give you the ability to strengthen and grow relationships you already have with existing customers. Our goal for you in sharing this information is to see you succeed, and get you more sustainable revenue for your company.

Here is one more item to be aware of before we begin. Know that this is not a 'how-to' guide, but rather a 'what to do' guide. You'll come to understand in reading this book that while marketing is vital to your company's future, it's also quite complicated and dynamic. It should be handled by experts. Your job in all this is knowing what to expect from your marketing team and seeing that it's delivered efficiently and effectively.

CHAPTER 1

AN OVERVIEW OF INBOUND MARKETING

Instead of the old outbound marketing methods of buying ads, buying email lists, and praying for leads, inbound marketing focuses on creating and promoting quality content that pulls people toward your company and product naturally when they are looking for information. By aligning the content you generate with your customer's interests, you'll naturally attract inbound traffic by publishing your content in the places your customers and prospects are searching for it. Your content will draw readers back to your website or a landing page, where you will convert them into sustainable customer relationships that you will continue to maintain over time.

Inbound marketing is about creating and sharing content with your ideal customers and prospects. By creating content to specifically appeal to your dream customers and then promoting it in a way that enables them to find it, you'll attract qualified prospects to your business and keep them coming back for more.

To give you a more informed idea of what is involved with inbound marketing, here are some major themes or common threads that exist in a successful inbound marketing strategy:

Content Creation + Content Distribution/Promotion: Targeted content that answers prospects' and customers' basic questions and needs that is shared far and wide, attracting as many sets of the right eyes as possible.

Lifecycle Marketing: Influential people who read and enjoy your content, and then share it with their own readers and/or followers so that it takes on a life of its own. These influential people are often referred to as "promoters", and having them share your content is a powerful way to lengthen your content's reach, giving your company greater exposure. Are you sharing your content with thought-leaders? If you believe they'll enjoy it and find it valuable, chances are, they'll share it with their own listeners or fans. Often, promoters start off as strangers. They could be any visitor to your website – a contact, a prospect, or even a customer. By using tools that track a visitor's actions and behaviors to build relationships with them, you can transform those strangers into promoters.

Personalization: Personalization is the ability to tailor your content to the wants and needs of the people who are viewing it. Technology exists today that tells us exactly who has been to your website, what their name is, and how often they visit. When they leave your website and return, their experience will be personalized specifically to them based on their previous visit. As we learn more about a visitor over time, messages are further personalized to meet their specific needs.

Multi-channel Marketing: Inbound marketing is multi-channel by nature because it approaches your viewers where they are, in the channel where they spend time and want to interact with you. It's beneficial, therefore, to produce your content and make it available in several forms – social media, blog posts, videos, podcasts, etc. to reach as many viewers as possible.

By promoting the right content in the right place at the right time (also known as targeted marketing), your marketing becomes relevant and helpful to your customers, not interruptive.

The Four Key Inbound Marketing Actions

Action #1: Attract

Don't attract just *any* traffic to your website, attract the *right* traffic. Attract the people who are most likely to become leads, and, ultimately, happy customers. Who are the "right" people?

Describe your ideal customers to create buyer personas.

Buyer personas are holistic ideals of what your perfect customers are really like, inside and out. Personas encompass their goals, challenges, pain points, common objections to products and services, as well as personal and demographic information shared among all members of that particular customer type. **Your personas are the people around whom your whole business is built.**

For instance, if you are a distributor of sporting goods, you would have several personas. They may include an owner of a small sporting goods storefront, a sport-specific shop owner, a buyer for a large sporting goods chain or department store, and an end user of your product line. When running your marketing campaigns, adapt your messaging to fit the needs of these different buyer personas.

What's difficult is knowing what will be of value to your readers' lives and not only their jobs; so by creating your buyer personas, you'll understand your readers better, and target your marketing more precisely.

Call it knowing your target market, call it knowing your customer, or call it having a crystal clear vision and unilateral understanding of who it is that buys from you. No matter the nomenclature, with a crystallized picture of WHO you are creating content for, the task of target marketing and content creation gets imminently easier.

When marketing without a buyer persona, people tend to create content from their own perspective. This often yields a limited arsenal of boring, company-centric content that will eventually repel the exact people you are trying to attract, so do not skip this step.

We've learned that company-centric content focused solely on how great your company, your products, or your achievements are doesn't get shared; and sharing is a key indicator of 'remarkability', meaning people will remark or comment on your content as they share. Creating content without targeting a strong persona will result in uninteresting, unremarkable, and unshared content. Content that appeals to your buyer persona(s) will get commented on and shared, and be noticed by more of your existing and potential customers.

When creating your buyer persona, it's necessary then to dig deep, past the obvious. What do you believe might keep them up at night? Is it anything to do with your product? Probably not, so get creative and think out of the box. For example, they may lose sleep worrying about things like:

- How they'll pay the mortgage on their store

- How they'll increase foot traffic and generate more revenue

- How they'll increase loyalty and repeat visits

- How they'll compete with the big box stores

- How they'll attract and retain the best talent

As you engage in the exercise of creating your buyer personas, you'll find yourself discovering a much stronger insight into their lives and minds. Doing so will give you a much better ability to create content that relates directly to them, catching and holding their attention longer and more often, eventually building and strengthening your bond with them and increasing their loyalty and trust in you.

How to Build Your Buyer Personas

Building your buyer personas is not difficult, but it does take time and creativity, which often is best served by a brain-storming session or two with some teammates. Follow these steps and you'll be well on your way.

1. Gather the team-members who have the best insight into your customer base for a brainstorming session. Perhaps enlist a member of your sales force, someone from customer service, and a receptionist or secretary who has a lot of interaction with

customers. Choose people who will be comfortable speaking freely amongst the group.

2. Start with the basics by answering some key questions, such as:

    - Who is your perfect customer? It's common for there to be several, but challenge yourselves to narrow down it down to one the first time around. Build out secondary personas later.

    - What are their typical demographics?

    - What are their key motivators in life, at work, or at play?

    - What are their biggest challenges and obstacles to success, at work or at play?

    - How do they consume information?

    - Who influences their decisions?

    These questions will help frame the starting point.

3. Give your persona a name (like Gus Golfshop or Debbie DepartmentStore) so that you talk about Gus and Debbie as though they were real people. You'll find it easier to identify with them this way.

4. Once you've got your first buyer persona fleshed out, move on to the next, until you've exhausted all permutations of your ideal customer.

Now you're better prepared to create content that will appeal to your personas.

As millennials move into buying roles in your customers' organizations, remember to include them when creating your buyer personas. There is no question the millennial generation will look online for everything they need – be it personal or for their organization. If your company is on the internet with a strong presence, answering their questions and providing whatever they're searching for, you're more likely to continue doing business with them.

This means that, not only will it be necessary to have a strategy that attracts millennials online, your company must also be in a position to serve up what they need, which inevitably means an e-commerce website is in your company's future. We won't get into e-commerce in this book, but we highly recommend that you explore using e-commerce as it matures into an economical and effective sales and marketing channel for your industry.

Now that you know who your buyer personas are, here's an overview of several of the tools you'll use to attract the right people to your website. Each one of these tools will be discussed in more detail throughout the book:

Blogging: Inbound marketing often starts with a good blog. When done well, a blog can be the single best way to attract new visitors to your website. Write about interesting, informative and educational content that speaks to your customers and prospects, and answers their questions.

SEO (or Search Engine Optimization): The majority of your customers will begin their buying process online, using a search engine to find answers to questions they have or solutions to problems they're working on. When your company appears prominently whenever and wherever they search, they'll find you easily and often, strengthening your position as an industry leader. Carefully and analytically choose your keywords, and then incorporate those keywords into your web pages and while creating your content. Include links around the terms your ideal buyers are searching for.

If your distribution company relies heavily on e-commerce, an investment in SEO is mandatory, often starting with paid search until your organic search optimization becomes more effective. Paid search is often referred to as SEM or Search Engine Marketing. To keep your costs down, and make your marketing efforts most effective, this is the time to enlist the assistance of third-party experts for keyword research and positioning. A well-planned search marketing strategy is instrumental to attracting new customers.

Website Pages: Your website pages are your digital storefront, so put your company's best face forward! Optimize your website with content that appeals to your ideal buyers, and transforms it into a beacon of helpful, interesting information that entices new visitors and existing customers to visit your pages again and again.

Social Media: Successful inbound strategies are all about remarkable content - and social media allows you to share valuable information on several pages around the web, engaging with your prospects and customers, and often putting a human face on your brand. With social media, interact on the networks where your ideal buyers spend their time. We'll dive deep into social media in later chapters, so for now, know that it's a necessity to your overall inbound marketing strategy.

Action #2: Convert

Once you've attracted visitors to your website, the next step is to convert those visitors into leads by gathering information about them. At the very least, you'll need their contact information; specifically, their email addresses.

Contact information is the most valuable currency there is to the online marketer. In order for your visitors to offer up that currency willingly, you'll need to offer them something as valuable, or more valuable, in return. That value or exchange of currency comes in the form of content, like e-books, whitepapers, videos, tip sheets, or whatever information would be interesting and valuable to your various buyer personas.

We'll expand on successful conversion strategies in future chapters. For now, though, here is a short list of some of the most common methods used to convert visitors into leads:

Lead Capture Forms: Visitors become leads when they fill out a form (also known as a lead capture box) on your website and submit their information. Optimize your form to make this step of the conversion process as easy as possible. Don't ask for too much information. A first name and email address should be enough for now. As the lead gets further down your sales funnel, an appropriate time will come to ask for more information.

Calls-to-Action: Calls-to-action are buttons or text links that encourage your visitors to take action. Phrases on buttons and links such as "Download a Whitepaper" or "Attend a Free Training Session" are common calls-to-action. If your company's web site does not have enough calls-to-action or your calls-to-action aren't enticing enough, you won't generate leads. Calls-to-action can be placed on your social media properties as well.

__Landing Pages__: When someone clicks on a call-to-action, they are sent to a landing page. A landing page is where the offer in the call-to-action is further promoted, and where the prospect then submits their contact information (usually via the lead capture form) that your sales team can use to begin a conversation with them. When website visitors fill out a form on a landing page for the first time, that visitor becomes a contact or lead.

__Contact Management__: Keep track of the leads you're converting in a centralized marketing database or CRM. Having all your data in one place helps you make sense from every interaction you've had with your contacts -- be it through email, a landing page, social media, or otherwise -- and will allow you to optimize your future interactions to more effectively attract, convert, and close your buyers (see below).

Action #3: Close

Once you've attracted the right visitors and converted the right leads, it's time to transform those leads into customers. How will you most effectively accomplish this feat? Here are some tools that will guide you and help ensure you're moving steadily down the path of closing the right leads at the right times:

__CRM:__ Customer Relationship Management (CRM) systems facilitate sales by tracking the behaviors of a prospect, ensuring you have the right information at your fingertips to better engage with prospects across every channel. A good CRM system will keep track of every detail about each contact, company, and deal in your pipeline, allowing you to easily access information on the right prospects at the right time.

Closed-loop Reporting: How do you know which marketing efforts are bringing in the best leads? Is your sales team effectively closing those best leads into customers? Improving and optimizing your marketing is much easier when you understand your marketing data and have the ability to measure each step or channel in your marketing funnel. Integration of a good reporting system with your CRM system will allow you to analyze how well your marketing and sales teams are playing together.

Email: What do you do if a visitor clicks on your call-to-action, fills out a landing page, or downloads your whitepaper, but still isn't ready to become a customer? It's likely this will be true for 99% of every visitor to your website and every person you come across via social media. As such, a series of emails focused on useful, relevant content can build trust with a prospect and either help them move closer to a buying decision, or at the very least, keep you top of mind for when they are ready to buy.

Email marketing is often an automated process, and it's an effective way to help cultivate a lead into a buyer. When set up properly, many industries have realized tremendous benefits from well-written, effective email marketing campaigns. The best email marketing systems are able to track reader behavior and report on who opened which emails and who clicked on which links. When the emails contain links with calls-to-action, it's valuable knowing which link(s) a viewer clicked on. This enables you to see what interests your readers and what does not.

Marketing Automation: A good marketing automation system will nurture your leads into sales readiness. This process involves creating email marketing and lead nurturing messages tailored to the needs and lifecycle stage of each individual lead. For example, if a visitor downloaded a whitepaper on a certain topic from you in the past, sending that lead a series of related emails would be effective. At the same time, if another visitor follows you on Twitter and visits product pages on your website from time to time, messaging for that visitor might reflect his specific interests instead. Tools that enable this behavior to be tracked and reported on can be costly, but because of their analytical features, it's fairly easy to measure their return on investment.

Action #4: Build Loyalty

A happy customer is a loyal customer, there's no doubt about it. But what makes customers (and prospects) most loyal?

Research has shown that in the distribution industry especially, when a customer has a problem or issue that needs resolving, they don't need a whole lot of fanfare or a dazzling experience to quell their unhappiness. They want the problem solved as quickly and efficiently as possible.

Customer loyalty comes from your knowing your customers, anticipating their issues and preventing problems from occurring in the first place. If a problem does occur, the first order of business is to listen. Customers with problems need to be heard and taken seriously in order to avoid any negative word-of-mouth marketing.

How do you know if a customer is unhappy? They don't always tell you, and in many cases, you may be the last to know.

The "inbound" way is all about providing remarkable content to your users that demonstrates that you are approachable and interested in what is going on with them. Are they happy? Are their needs met? Is there anything else you can do for them? Show them that you care through what you share on the internet.

Just because someone has already written you a check doesn't mean it's okay to forget about them! Quite the opposite. Use inbound marketing tactics to continue to engage with them. Eventually you may even upsell your current customer base, converting them into happy promoters of your organization and your products and services.

This tactic is often forgotten, and usually comes to light only after a company notices they are losing too many customers. The best practice is to put this tactic into place immediately. Build it directly into your marketing funnel as a step that is mandatory after the sale. A few ways to accomplish this include:

Surveys: The best way to learn what your users want or what they think about your company is by asking them. Solicit feedback and use surveys to ensure you're providing customers with what they want and need.

Social Monitoring: Keep track of the social conversations that matter to you most – your customers'. Listen out for your customers' questions, comments, likes, and dislikes – and reach out to them with relevant content.

Inbound marketing covers each and every step taken, tool used, and lifecycle stage traveled through on the road from stranger to customer. It empowers your company to attract visitors, convert leads, close customers, and impress promoters. Inbound marketing takes some work; make a conscious effort to do it by using tools and applications that create and deliver content that appeals to precisely the right people (your buyer personas) in the right places (channels) at the right times (lifecycle stages).

CHAPTER 2

OPTIMIZING YOUR WEBSITE

Just because you built it, doesn't mean they will come. You may have the most beautiful website on the internet, with lots of funky bells and whistles, but if you're not attracting traffic, your website is about as effective as a billboard in the desert.

Your website is your company's virtual storefront. It's the first place buyers go to learn about your company, products and service, and it's the place you'll drive your traffic to through your inbound marketing efforts. Your website, when set up properly, will get more leads, simplify your sales process, increase repeat customers, and as a result, improve the profitability of your business.

Today's buyers wish to consume information when they want and how they want, and they want to be educated instead of sold to. For this reason, your website is now a considerable factor in your company's sales funnel.

To attract visitors, it's going to take more than an inbound marketing strategy. Optimize your website as well. Search engine optimization, or SEO, is just as important to getting your website discovered via search engines like Google, Bing, and Yahoo.

The traditional approach to SEO involves two sets of tactics: on-page SEO and off-page SEO. On-page SEO is the strategic implementation of keywords <u>on</u> your website, including in the website's page titles, its headers, its meta descriptions, and the content on the page.

Off-page SEO, in comparison, refers to improving your website's overall authority <u>elsewhere</u> on the web, which is determined by which *other websites* are linking to you. The goal with off-page SEO is to attract inbound links (also known as "backlinks") from relevant, authoritative websites that matter to large audiences.

The State of SEO Today *(which will probably be different tomorrow)*

While on-page and off-page SEO are essential concepts, they are rooted in an approach that is falling by the wayside. In the past, the goal of SEO was to impress (or almost trick) the search engines by overusing keywords and fake backlinks so that the search engines rewarded websites with higher rankings, with the ultimate goal being to achieve the coveted number one spot in the search results for one or more target keyword.

Today, search engines are much smarter. They can tell the difference between websites that are designed to game the system, and they are much better at recognizing legitimate websites that are providing relevant high-quality content. Search engines measure things like bounce rates (i.e., how long someone stays at your website) and numbers of click-throughs (i.e., how many links they click on your website), so today the most successfully-designed SEO is about optimizing content for the real searchers or viewers, not the search engines.

Many business owners don't understand the importance of having a website that's optimized and drawing a lot of traffic. They feel that because their customers aren't buying from them on the internet, they shouldn't be concerned with building traffic to their website. Years ago that may have been true, but today it's no longer the case. In an age where every need is searched on and addressed on the internet, your customers and prospects who have a problem or need will first search for a solution to that need on the internet. Your website appearing at the top of the search engines to solve their problem is crucial.

It's no longer just about selling on the internet. In the business to business world, selling on the internet is still a fairly new concept, as you probably know. However, providing solutions to people's problems quickly and clearly is not new. Today, when your customers or prospects have dilemmas they need to resolve, they WILL turn to the internet first to solve their problems. If your product is the answer to their dilemma, they will learn about it much quicker if the information is online instead of tucked into your catalog or filed away with your sales materials. If your product and a competitor's product are both an answer to their dilemma, your product should be the solution they find more quickly and easily.

According to a study done by Pew Research Center, three technological revolutions have occurred that have caused internet use to grow exponentially, and this research points to the fact that your customers are looking for their solutions online.

First, the research tells us that the availability of broadband in the average home has contributed greatly to an increase in the way people get information and share it with each other, affecting everything from users' basic social relationships to the way they work, learn, and care for themselves. The speed of internet connectivity has increased dramatically, and as people adopt higher-speed, always-on connections, they've become different internet users than they were even two or three years ago. They spend more time online, performing more activities, watching more media, and creating more media themselves.

Second, mobile connectivity through smartphones and tablets has made "anytime-anywhere" access to information a reality for the vast majority of Americans. Mobile devices have changed the way people think about how and when they can communicate and gather information by making just-in-time and real-time encounters possible. They have also affected the way people allocate their time and attention.

Pew Research Center also found that Americans still find that obtaining information digitally is most beneficial despite the "ceaseless flow of commentary about information overload." They predict that in 2015, Americans will consume "an average of 15.5 hours of media per person per day of 30 different kinds of media in video, print, audio, and gaming formats."

Third, the rise of social media and social networking has affected the way people think about their friends, acquaintances, and even strangers. People have always had social networks of family and friends that helped them. The new reality is that as people create social networks in technology spaces, those networks are often much bigger and more diverse than before.

"Social media allows people to plug into those networks more readily and more broadly – making them persistent and pervasive in ways that were once unimaginable. One of the major impacts we need to remember here is that the traditional boundaries between private and public, between home and work, between being a consumer of information and producer of it are now forever blurred." *(Credit: PewInternet.org)*

So while many business to business customers are not buying from distributors online yet, this research indicates that distributors still must increase their focus on using the internet to reach their customers and prospects, and they should consider their website as the hub or center for all their online activity. A user-friendly website is probably the most powerful marketing tool a company can have for efficient and effective lead generation.

When your website is laid out in a way that makes information easy to find, visitors will tend to spend more time there, which is something search engines monitor and reward by ranking you higher in search results. Couple that with an effective lead capture campaign, and you've got a winning combination.

But it's only a winning combination when your customers and prospects can find it. That's where good SEO and SEM (Search Engine Marketing) factor in.

For example, Performance Foodservice, a food distributor from Richmond, recently redesigned and relaunched their new website, but didn't stop there. To start, they filled their new website with big, beautiful images of delicious food, and each image links to information that would be helpful to their customers. This helpful information and their bold images are there to impress visitors and keep them on the website. Phrases like "Custom Solutions", "Learn More About", "Grow With Us", and "Build Your Business" are prevalent throughout their website, enticing their visitors to explore further and further.

They've also got multiple menus on their home page, which make it very easy for visitors to find what they're looking for and discover new things as well.

Performance Foodservice also invested a lot of time and effort in both their social media efforts and their video marketing efforts. They've got a well-tended-to main page on Facebook in addition to a Facebook page tab (i.e., an additional page) solely devoted to videos from both their own marketing team (via the Performance Foodservice Test Kitchen) as well as videos featuring their manufacturers. Their Performance Foodservice Test Kitchen is a brilliant marketing strategy. They're showing their ideal customers how to use their products most effectively. Perhaps that's something your distribution company can do, too.

The company also built a gorgeous blog. It's self described as a blog "For Foodies, By Foodies". Here's what they say about their blog, FoodCentric.com:

"FoodCentric is a collection of articles, recipes, trends and ideas for the inquisitive foodie and food service professional. Our content is brought to you by the many chefs, sales representatives, suppliers, and food enthusiasts of Performance Foodservice, one of the largest food distributing companies in the US." Notice there is nothing "salesy" in that description.

The following paragraph is taken from their company description. Notice how it's written with an emphasis on their customers, making it clear that their customers are of the utmost importance to them:

"Distribution is only part of our story. Customers also tap into our expertise for advice on improving their operations. We offer our customers suggestions on menu analysis and development, product selection, and operational strategies. By providing high-quality products and superior customer service, our team builds long-lasting relationships with our customers."

This is a company that understands the importance of putting the customer first. Spending time on Performance Foodservice's website and blog is an enjoyable experience. Because they've got what it takes to hold a customer's or prospect's attention for a good long time, search engines will recognize that and reward them with strong rankings.

In a recent interview with the popular publication, *Modern Distribution Magazine*, Angela Rodenburgh, Marketing Director for plastics distributor Redwood Plastics explained that the benefits from investing in an online platform go beyond being able to sell products online. She went on to explain that one of the biggest benefits comes from developing a place to engage your customer base. According to Rodenburgh, tools such as online chat, social media and search engine marketing appear to have paid off for her company. In the interview she stated that "There's a huge opportunity with the way people are looking for information, and if you don't see that opportunity, (you're) really missing out on a large audience. As the younger generations continue to move into purchasing roles, that opportunity will continue to grow." (*Credit: Modern Distribution Management*)

Getting Started With SEO: 5 Elements of Optimization

We've come across many websites that are missing some of these basic elements of SEO, and so it's worth devoting a few pages in this book to educate you on what to look for and correct on your own website. If you're missing any of these five elements, you're losing traffic, and your website should be corrected right away.

Element #1: Page Titles

A page title is the text you see at the top of your browser window when viewing a web page. It's also the title of a page that is presented in search engine results.

The page title is found and edited in your website's HTML code. It is the text that is surrounded with the <title> tag on each page, and it's significant because when search engines visit your page, they check to see if the title matches the content on the page itself. If it does, you get a boost in that highly coveted, ever-elusive remedy we call Google juice!

Your page titles should be written to adequately describe and align with the page's content. Relevant keywords should be included and placed as close to the beginning of the title as possible. Your page's title should be less than 70 characters long, and it should include your company name if possible toward the end. Each page should have a unique page title.

Element #2: Meta Descriptions

A meta description is a short summary that is written for each web page, and search engines display the meta descriptions in search results after the title.

Meta descriptions don't count toward search engine rankings, but they are still incredibly useful. Because they appear in your company's search engine results, meta descriptions should include compelling copy that accurately describes your page's content, enticing the searcher to click.

Element #3: Headings

If a piece of text appears larger or more prominent than the other text on a web page, chances are it's part of a heading. You can verify this by checking the HTML code of your website and looking for text with an <h1>, <h2>, or <h3> tag surrounding it.

Both search engines and searchers alike tend to pay more attention to headings in comparison to regular paragraph text. Headings act as guides or sight words for what's contained on the page. Your headings should include keywords whenever possible to make it easy for the reader to find what they're looking for, and they should truly reflect what's sitting on the page. Include keywords and keyword phrases, but don't over do it. Search engines will compare your headings with the rest of the text on the page, and if there isn't a sufficient balance between the two, you may be penalized and rank lower in the search engines.

Keywords in <h1> tags give the text that follows more weight than <h2> or <h3> tags. Including too many headings dilutes the importance of keywords in other headings, so we recommend using the <h1> tag only once on each page. If the page is text-heavy (like a blog post), then use a few <h2> or <h3> tags as paragraph titles.

Element #4: Images

Images on a web page can enhance your reader's experience. Similar to a header, they lead people in the right direction through your website, and break up text that may appear too heavy. Including relevant images in your website is a fairly easy thing to do and understand. However, there are still certain guidelines to follow.

For example, each picture on your sight should have accompanying text attached to it. For whatever reason, images on your website may fail to render or appear to a visitor, and if this happens, the text that is attached to the picture will still present the idea regardless of the picture's appearance. The "alt text" HTML attribute is what's used to provide relevant text descriptions of your images. This will help ensure that visitors can still understand the information you're presenting, should your images fail to appear.

The image file names should include keywords. Search engines pick up on these file names, and doing so will help you draw in relevant traffic from image searches. The words in the file names should be separated with a hyphen (-), not an underscore (_). Search engines recognize the hyphen as a space but they do not recognize the underscore. When an underscore is used to separate multiple words, search engines will read them as one long word.

Lastly, don't use images excessively. More pictures can slow down the loading of your page, and have a negative impact on both user experience and the website's search engine optimization.

Element #5: URL Structure

The URL of a web page is simply its web address. URL *structure* refers to how the text in a URL is organized, as well as how the different URLs on your website interact with one another. When examining the structure of your website's URLs, there are a few best practices to keep in mind.

Keywords should be used in your URL structure, and if there is more than one word (for example, www.yourwebsite.com/information-and-resources), separate the words with a hyphen, similar to how you would with your images. Similar to how the image files are read, doing so will let the search engines know that the page is about both information and resources. If someone is searching for information about your company, or they are searching for resources from your company, more than likely, both times, the search engines will return that page.

Also similar to image file names, don't allow the words to run into each other, and don't separate them with an underscore. Doing so will be misconstrued by the search engines as one long non-word (i.e., informationandresources).

The URL structure should describe what's on the page or what the page is about. Often, we see URLs with numbers or abbreviations in them. Using numbers or abbreviations that have no meaning will result in a less than great experience for your website visitor, which may leave them frustrated and moving on to your competitor's website. The URLs for your company's product pages should each contain the product name and not the product number, unless people will be searching for your products by their product number.

Whenever possible, when updating or cancelling a webpage, a 301 redirect should be used. A 301 redirect forwards an old URL to a new one. Do this when you change the URL of a page on your website. A common mistake is not applying a 301 redirect between yoursite.com and www.yoursite.com. This can be quite a problem from an SEO standpoint, because search engines will give separate credit to both versions of your website, diluting your "Google juice".

Optimizing for Mobile

The topic of mobile marketing is tossed around frequently in marketing circles, often with many different intended meanings.

While mobile marketing can mean many things, there is one primary thing that business owners who wish to take advantage of mobile marketing must know regarding the true intention of what mobile marketing is all about. It is the practice of making sure your website looks terrific and works perfectly on a mobile device. If you've ever pulled up a website on either your smartphone or your tablet and it did not display correctly – leading to a "pinch and zoom" interaction, you know the importance of getting this right.

While there are a few different options for providing a great mobile web experience, such as creating a separate mobile website or launching an app, the best option -- from an optimization standpoint -- is to use what's called a responsive website.

A responsive website uses the same URL and HTML code across all devices: desktops, laptops, tablets, and smartphones. The only thing that changes is the CSS, which is a programming language that describes the style and formatting of a web page.

The CSS allows the content on your website to adapt to different screen sizes, always delivering a great viewing and browsing experience to your visitor. What's more, Google prefers responsive design to other mobile technologies because it allows for more efficient crawling and indexing. Search engines have begun penalizing websites that aren't responsive. For example, if you don't have a mobile website, it's possible your site won't appear at all in mobile searches.

If your online strategy does not already include a mobile website, we suggest you add one right away. Mobile usage (smartphones and tablets) have overtaken the traditional computer for internet access and especially for search. Having a well-structured mobile-friendly website or a responsive website will ensure that when your customer or prospect is looking for your information on their smartphone or tablet, not only will they find your website, but they'll find the information they are looking for easily and quickly.

CHAPTER 3

CREATING CONTENT

Today more than ever, content truly is king when it comes to being found online.

Once you've optimized your website for your visitors as well as for the search engines, it will be time to create good, valuable content. Content is the fuel that drives your internet marketing. It's the foundation or cornerstone of your entire marketing strategy. It's what makes you better than your competition, what differentiates you from the rest, and quite possibly will become part of the legacy of your organization for future generations.

Your content should tell the story of your company in a way that makes it attractive and interesting. It should be reflective of the overall personality of the owners of the company, demonstrate your company's true culture, and even reflect your belief system. It is from your content that the majority of people will learn about you, so keep it interesting, perhaps fun, and definitely sincere. It's also your opportunity to be center stage and demonstrate the caliber of your expertise and position yourself as a thought-leader in your industry.

The ultimate goal of a good content marketing strategy is to attract the customers and prospects you prefer to work with, and perhaps not attract the companies that wouldn't be a good fit. It's the best, most effective and lasting way to reach your ideal customers and share with them the kind of information that will result in their knowing you better, liking you, and eventually trusting you more than any of your competitors to the point where they won't do business with anyone but you.

When you create valuable, high-quality relevant content targeted toward specific, well-defined audiences, you'll do more than attract visitors to your website. You'll attract the **right** visitors, who are likely to convert into leads (and eventually, customers).

What's more, content will help considerably with your website's SEO. (Remember "off-page" SEO from the previous chapter?) Creating and distributing content is the best way to earn those valuable inbound links that can boost your search rankings and help improve your website's discoverability.

Lastly, one of the biggest benefits derived from creating good valuable content is it will build your platform as an expert in your field or industry. It's an opportunity to show and share your knowledge for the betterment of others, which is a win-win all around. As your business changes, with new clients, products and solutions, your content strategy will be the first method to inform the marketplace about this information. When prospects with a similar need to your clients search for solutions to their problems, they will find your content. When you provide information that helps others, in all likelihood, readers will return again for more.

Creating and sharing interesting, relevant and valuable information will turn your website from an average website into a true resource (think library) that fills a need, and generates massive traffic.

Blogging for Business

A blog makes your website more dynamic by automatically injecting new content every time you publish an article. Search engines reward higher rankings to websites that consistently add fresh content, and these higher rankings translate into new visitors and leads for your business. Blog posts can be interactive, allowing readers to leave comments, and giving you an opportunity to create an ongoing dialogue with your prospects and customers.

It's an opportunity to share your stories. Originally blogs were very personal, written in the first person, but now there are company blogs, either with several writers, or authored by the company persona. Blogs have evolved from a personal "web log" to a communication platform for a company for latest news, press releases and client stories. When you blog, though, take off your hat as a business owner or marketing manager and try to think like a magazine publisher. Keep in mind that the goal of your business blog should be to publish **valuable, non-promotional information**, much in the way a column or an article in an industry magazine would. Writing non-promotional information is most difficult for business owners to do, so don't be frustrated if you miss the mark your first few tries out of the gate.

A blog gives customers and prospects who read it an excellent opportunity to truly know you as a persona, so be genuine. This is an opportunity for you to begin building a virtual relationship with your readers, who will be made up of customers and prospects.

Ideally, folks will choose to do business with you because they know, like and trust you (either personally or as a business), and this is a great opportunity to begin that process.

Also, be careful of the words you are using. Avoid industry jargon that only your employees would understand. Instead, think of the words your customers would use to describe what they need or are looking for, include those phrases in your blogging language. After all, those are the phrases people will likely be searching on, so those are the phrases that belong on your pages.

What Do You Write About?

Most business blogs start with a purpose. What are you trying to educate your industry and potential customers about? **This education is not about your company or your product, by the way.** Rather, it should be about common industry issues, the problems your customers and potential customers face and, sometimes, the solutions your product or service offer to tackle these challenges. Keep the slant more toward the solution and less toward how great your product is. Remember to keep it customer-centric.

A commonly used tactic to start blogging is to answer the ten most frequently asked questions you get from prospective new customers. Do this once a week for ten weeks and you have the foundation of a successful blog. Once those first ten weeks are over, check out your blogging analytics to see which articles resonate most with your audience. If two or three of the posts received a significantly higher number of views, shares, likes and inbound links, expand on those topics in future blog posts.

Another way to identify blogging topics is to make a list of the most common issues your prospects and clients are struggling with, whether your product or service is the solution or not. If you have an opinion on the subject or can offer some helpful advice, do so. Your opinion and advice is valuable, and if you solve someone's problem by revealing it, you will long be remembered.

Keep your eyes open for topics of interest and industry news in trade publications. These can be a great source of ideas to write about. So can social conversations. Read through the LinkedIn pages and Facebook pages of your customers, your competitors and other thought leaders in your industry. Doing so will enlighten you as to what people are interested in and talking about or struggling with. Speak to your sales force and the staff who spend time in the trenches with your customers. They're often tuned in to what your customers may be struggling with.

Remember to let your expertise and especially your passion shine through in your blog content.

Key Components of a Great Blog Post

A great blog post should ultimately be helpful, inspiring and clever. Some injected humor is always helpful as well. The actual content will of course come from you, your knowledge and your experiences and opinions. As you craft your blog posts, however, keep the following key components in mind.

<u>**A Compelling Title:**</u> A blog post's title is the first thing people will see, so it should clearly indicate what the article is about. Clarity and specificity will attract readers and prompt them to share the post with their networks.

Well-Written and Formatted Text: The body of your post should be well-written and formatted in a way that makes it easy to read. Consider using headings and bullet points to break up the content into sections. Always have a coworker or a friend review the post before you publish.

Multimedia Content: Relevant multimedia content can make a blog post more memorable and fun to read. It also helps to break up the text to make it more pleasing to the eye. Aim to add at least one relevant image per blog post. Slideshow presentations, video, and infographics are examples of other multimedia content to feature.

Links: Include in-text links to relevant content, helping readers dig deeper into the resources they are most interested in. Your links can, naturally, point to your own internal pages and landing pages to help you generate more leads from your content.

Call-to-Action (CTA): Each and every blog post you publish should include a relevant call-to-action in the article to help boost lead generation.

Generating Leads With Blogging

Business blogging presents a fantastic platform for attracting organic traffic and engaging with your audience. However, a step that most bloggers miss, and the primary goal of your business blog, is to drive conversions. To achieve this goal, add calls-to-action to your posts and have them link to landing pages that provide downloadable access to more in-depth learning materials, such as e-books or webinars. Include CTAs both in the sidebar of your blog as well as on every individual post you publish.

Other Content Strategies and Tactics that Generate Leads

While it's a great place to start and probably most prevalent, blog content isn't the only type of content to create to be successful with internet marketing. Here are some examples of other popular media, all of which should always be accompanied with a relevant call-to-action:

Articles: Articles are like blog posts that can be shared on public forums, generating interest in your subject matter and your company. They should contain links back to your website, preferably to a landing page with a special offer and a lead capture box.

E-books: Like a whitepaper, an e-book is also similar to an educational report. The difference, however, is that an e-book presents information in a visually attractive, reader-friendly format. The best written e-books are both informative and entertaining, sometimes even interactive. They contain more of a collegial tone, and often feature chunky pictures and sections of text to facilitate a quick read through.

Infographics: An Infographic is a reasonably new, fun and fast way to convey a lot of information using images in a visually aesthetic way that doesn't require a lot of reading. They often help simplify a complicated subject or turn a boring subject into something more interesting. Infographics are best known for the richness of the data they contain and their ability to educate. Infographics can be a terrific way to build brand awareness because they are very visual and interactive, making them memorable and shareable for most readers.

<u>Podcasts</u>: Podcasts are like videos, but without the picture. They're great for those of you who are camera shy, and technically, they're available via subscription, which means they're automatically delivered to your contacts' device, so the hurdle of your audience having to retrieve them doesn't exist. According to content marketing guru, Jay Baer, "More than any other content format, podcasting is poised to explode because it's the one type of content you can consume while also doing something else."

<u>Press Releases</u>: A press release is a brief summary or update written about your company's news and activities that is aimed toward the press. Press releases are similar to news articles in that they inform the public, but they're prepared in a specific, universally-accepted format that is clear, concise and quickly conveys a message. At one time, press releases were powerful in driving traffic to a website; however, while they're still commonly used, they're no longer as effective.

<u>Videos</u>: Online videos continue to rise as the content of choice. According to Cisco, video will account for 69% of all consumer internet traffic by 2017. There's no question that video is the future of content marketing. A video can be a full-blown production or a simple sound bite captured on your webcam. Statistics have shown that the investment in production rarely has an impact on its value. In other words, the value is in the content or message you're conveying, not in the video's production.

<u>Webinars</u>: Webinars are a great way to reach a large audience and share your expertise. They give you tremendous visibility, and position you as a thought-leader and an expert in your industry. They are interactive and allow tremendous engagement, and as a result, the timeline for your audience to get to know and like you is significantly reduced. Despite webinars having a high perceived value, today's technology makes them very easy to conduct.

Whitepapers: Whitepapers are educational reports or research papers, usually written around something industry-specific, and filled with relevant statistics. Whitepapers are a great opportunity for you and your company to demonstrate thought leadership and industry expertise.

Any of these robust forms of content can be used for lead generation, and therefore can be used to feed your business conversions. Although it's a resource that takes some time and effort to put together, they will provide the type of value visitors are looking for. It has the power to achieve your overall goal in creating content and generating a lead based on its value.

The offers you produce should not be randomly selected. Good marketing analytics should direct you to the types of content that attract your target audience. For instance, if a whitepaper on HVAC installation brought you more leads and sales than a webinar on the same topic, focus on creating more text-based content.

A common perception that prevents people from beginning the practice of content creation is that they believe it requires a lot of time and discipline. The truth is, it will require an investment of time and discipline, but there are ways to share the effort.

Perhaps you have a budding writer in your company who enjoys putting pen to paper. For that person, content generation may not feel like a burden and will not require discipline. Or, you could appoint a marketing team to share the writing, or even outsource the writing to an outside agency. Regardless of who does it, it needs to get done and it should be done well.

Making the Most from Your Content

Whenever possible, build up your arsenal of evergreen content. Evergreen content is content that remains "fresh" and timely, and as a result, is always relevant. It is not time sensitive. Evergreen content can be made up of instructional webinars about your products, guides, or anything else that won't eventually be outdated. When content is evergreen, the pressure of replacing it with something new is somewhat relieved.

Repurposing your content is another tactic to keep handy in your quiver. Content creation, of course, starts with an idea and the decision to share that idea. Repurposing, also known as multi-channel marketing, speaks to the decision of how the content will be shared. As mentioned above, the idea can be shared a variety of ways, through a blog post or a white paper, a video, a social media post, a podcast, an email, an article, etc. Here's how you do it most effectively and efficiently.

Create your content in a logical way, so that it can then be shared in many other forms to reach as many audiences as possible. As overwhelming as it sounds, it's very simple. Here's how: Say you have a great idea to share, and you start with something as simple as recording a 2 or 3-minute video on your iPhone or webcam. Once the video has been created, the audio can be stripped out and used as a podcast. It can also be transcribed into a blog post.

If you create several blog posts that are along the same theme, weave them together to create an article or a whitepaper. Then share each one of these media forms on your website, on YouTube or on public article spaces, and then shared even further through posts on Facebook, tweets on Twitter and through posts and group discussions on LinkedIn.

Promoting Your Content

Content promotion can be complicated and it may cost you some money – all the more reason to have good analytics in place. It used to be that if your content was optimized for the search engines, sent to an appropriate email list, and then broadcast via social media, a good amount of traffic would be drawn to your website within a reasonable timeframe. Unfortunately, that's no longer the case.

Because more and more content is competing for your viewers' attention today, put as much effort into promoting your content as you do creating it. Think about your methods of promotion before generating the actual content. Think about who the audience is and how you'll reach them. Decide whether you'll invest in paid promotion. Only pay to promote content that you are confident is outstanding, however. Do not pay to promote mediocre content.

Here are some effective ways to promote your content. All of these tactics work well, although some are more difficult or cost more than others. Be sure that, no matter what, any content you generate ends with a call-to-action back to your website so that you capture the lead.

Advertorials: Advertorials are articles that appear in publications and look as thought the article were part of the publication, but in truth are paid advertisements. These pieces are almost always denoted with the word "sponsored".

Bylined Articles: Bylined articles result when media outlets invite company executives with a specific expertise to write for them. This could be a one-time event, or a regular series of articles.

Content Discovery Networks: These are networks that you pay to carry your content, getting it in front of large audiences. This is the covert advertising that you'll see at the bottom of popular pages like Yahoo with a heading along the lines of "From Around the Web".

Email Marketing: Email marketing remains a highly effective mode of promotion, provided you have a substantial list of contacts. You can use email marketing to build an existing list by adding a suggestion to the bottom of each of your emails that suggests to the recipient that they share your message with anyone else who may benefit from your message. You can also use email marketing to segment your list. You'll find much more about email marketing in an upcoming chapter.

Media Relations: Placing your content in well-known publications will indeed drive brand awareness, traffic and conversions. To do this, however, it usually is necessary to employ a PR or Marketing specialist who has a relationship with a media entity to gain entrance into the more popular publications.

Social Influencers: We talked about social influencers or "promoters" earlier in the book. Have your content promoted by someone in your industry who has a big following or mailing list. It may happen organically, they may stumble across you and like what they see. You might also ask them directly to share your blog post with their followers or tweet or post about your company or your product.

Social Media Advertising: Looking for a quick way to generate more likes, followers and re-tweets? The major social media channels each now feature various forms of advertising which, when done correctly, can be cost effective and very well targeted.

Social Media Broadcasting: The companies that embraced social media years ago quickly and easily got in front of their audiences with little to no out-of-pocket costs. They only had to post, and 80-90% of their audience would see it. Now that the major social media channels have gone public, revenue has become a factor, and social media channels limit a brand's reach in an effort to generate more advertising dollars. As a result, social media is no longer as effective *organically* as it once was. In order to use social media to grow your audience, you must either be patient and disciplined as we've been discussing, or plan to pay for advertising. The good news is that, as mentioned above, social media advertising is still a good investment. We'll discuss social media broadcasting more fully in the next chapter.

Syndication: Similar to what was originally the cornerstone of the newspaper business, you may have your content syndicated across the internet and available at multiple websites in addition to your own. Doing so will increase your exposure and strengthen your foothold on being seen as a thought-leader. Depending on which sites carry your material, this strategy may also build up the back links to your website, which will help raise it in the search engine rankings.

CHAPTER 4

USING SOCIAL MEDIA TO ATTRACT LEADS AND PROMOTE YOUR CONTENT

Wholesale distribution companies, like most business-to-business companies, often struggle with how to use social media to grow their brand. It's new, it's evolving, and it's difficult to understand not only how social media can play a role in your business, but whether it's worth investing time and talent, and then know how to measure its success.

If you find, like most distribution executives, the whole "social media thing" overwhelming and non-intuitive, you are not alone. The truth is, though, if you're not using social media, you're missing out on a very powerful opportunity to connect with your prospects and existing clients, as well as with your very own employees and future employees as well. Social media will also help you attract new business and new talent to your organization, while at the same time, strengthening your brand's online presence. Social media makes you approachable and human. Your business may be business-to-business, but in actuality, business always will boil down to P2P, or person to person.

Your goal in using social media, of course, is to attract more business, but social media has a softer side. It's the "stuff" that comes before the lead generation. It's about reach, awareness, creating buzz, gauging customer satisfaction and overall engagement. These are some of the necessary stepping stones to lead generation, and they should not be ignored.

Like any other form of marketing, social media requires a well-thought-out strategy. Because it's technology-driven, it can be easily measured (versus print media), and because it grows "organically", it requires a strong, long-term commitment. It's here to stay, and for distribution companies who wish to stay competitive, it is necessary to get on board in order to expand or even maintain the status quo of your brand or recruit from the up and coming (and growing) and hard-to-attract millennial generation.

If for nothing else, the increase in search engine rankings alone that your company will generate by having a Google+ page, a Facebook page, a Twitter page and a LinkedIn page makes it well worth your while to invest the time and effort it takes to set them up. Every single time you share a post or tweet on Twitter it creates a link back to your website, raising your company's profile in the search engines. This is an incredibly powerful concept.

Distribution companies like Grainger, WinWholesale, and Redwood Plastics have found great success with their social media efforts. In an age where customer-centric focus is imperative in order to remain competitive, using social media is incredibly effective in learning what your customers want from you and what your customers think about you, and in having the ability to respond to them immediately.

In a recent interview with *Modern Distribution Management*, Sarif Renno, Social Media Manager at Grainger was quoted as saying "Social media is extremely important. Customers now have a bigger, more public voice than they ever did before, and they are shifting the way they communicate. Brands that wish to stay relevant and connected to customers must be willing to adopt social channels, add value through a service or smart content and listen – really listen – to what customers are saying."

Grainger is doing a great job at maintaining a powerful social media presence, but, you may be thinking "of course they are, they're Grainger. They're a huge company and seem to have unlimited manpower." You may be wondering how to possibly compete.

At WinWholesale's Facebook page, you'll find them using a combination of helpful tips targeted toward their end users, sometimes mixed with some humor to make their message more memorable. This is a tactic that anyone with a little creativity can do just as well. Keeping it simple and memorable is the most effective way to engage the widest audience possible, and doing so will keep you top of mind whenever a customer or prospect is looking for a supplier they know, like and trust.

With today's technology, even the smallest of companies can compete with a Grainger or a WinWholesale when it comes to social media. There are so many tools to take advantage of to share your messages and help you listen to what people are saying. Most of these tools are free or very affordable, although they can seem rather complicated; one of the most difficult hurdles to achieve in your social media effort is deciding which tools to use, and then learning how to use them.

The downside to using technology is that, like all technology, it changes, and staying current with the changes can be difficult. For example, if your company uses a tool that automatically posts to Facebook, and then Facebook changes the rules, that tool may no longer work for Facebook posting, in which case, a new tool will be needed.

For example, years ago Facebook had an agreement with Twitter and allowed an app (fancy name for a computer program) to post whatever we posted on Facebook to also automatically post to Twitter. When that agreement fell apart or the app broke (we don't know what happened really), we found ourselves scrambling for a new way to auto-post to Twitter. Then they reinstated the app. Go figure. There are dozens of incidents like this that have occurred over the past 5 years, and we expect that there will be dozens more to come. It's the nature of the business.

An alternative to mastering the technology is to outsource your social media and marketing efforts to an expert. In a world of telecommuting and entrepreneurship, it's not difficult to find reputable marketing consulting companies like ours to delegate your marketing efforts to. This solution gives you the best of both worlds -- access to the most powerful, knowledgeable marketing experts available while literally saving tens of thousands of dollars in time and money trying to do it internally.

Marketing consulting companies like ours make it our daily business to stay on top of and ahead of not only our clients', but the marketing that our clients' competitors are conducting as well. A good marketing agency will act as your eyes and ears in the marketplace, and with your collaboration, also function as your marketing mouthpiece, ensuring that your messages are heard by the right people in the right places at the right time.

Regardless of who handles your company's social media, let's take a look at what to share on social media, and why. To start with, the idea is to engage with your customers and prospects. Put your feet in their shoes when deciding what to share. Your customers and prospects, while they may love you dearly, are going to be bombarded with marketing messages all day long, every day, and the messages they pay the most attention to will be the messages that answer one very important question the right way: "What's in it for them?"

When you're crafting your messages, use that question as a test. Writing about your brand is fine, but when you do, ask yourself, "What's in this message for my customer?" You may have news about your company, but again, ask yourself "how does this news affect my customer?"

At first, it may sound almost impossible to approach your messaging from this direction. After all, why would your customer care or how would they benefit from news about your brand? But after a while, with a strong, long-term commitment and the right focus, you'll become more familiar with seeing things from your customers' and prospects' perspectives, and you'll learn how to present information to them so they can clearly see how they benefit from your services and products without your sounding like you're tooting your own horn.

On the flip side, it's incredibly useful to use social media to listen to what your customers are saying. Through their posts and shares and follows, you'll learn who and what your customers and prospects like and dislike, and often gain insight into their loyalties (as in, toward your competitors) as well. It can be as simple as visiting their Facebook pages, following their Twitter feeds, or joining their LinkedIn groups. Leverage these tools to keep tabs on what people are talking about, to see where they're spending time (both personally and professionally), and to build relationships with them by engaging and getting to know them better, and allowing them to get to know you better. This kind of knowledge can be valuable as you craft your buyer personas.

It is worth briefly mentioning that, many a company has had its reputation ruined via social media because social media does give individuals a very loud voice. So while we encourage you to use social media to build your brand and foster stronger relationships, also use social media to monitor your own reputation. Truthfully, it's almost always in the business-to-consumer world where we see companies raked through the mud by unhappy customers – we rarely see it in a business-to-business situation. However, if your company has end products or end services that affect individual consumers, you're not immune from somebody's tirade, so it's imperative that you keep your online presence squeaky clean.

There are too many people who thrive on and perpetuate negative press. If and when such negativity lands on your doorstep, nip it in the bud immediately and properly. We cannot stress enough how crucial to your reputation it is to take immediate swift action to remedy any such situation, and ALWAYS consult an outside, third-party expert in the process.

Trying to remedy a negative press situation yourself is an incredibly bad idea. Emotions run high, perspective is lost, and your company can suffer tremendous losses through having a bad reputation. It can not only affect your future sales, but it can affect your standings in the search engines (negative press will always have more clicks than positive). It will affect your ability to recruit new employees or investors, and it certainly will affect your state of mind and ability to sleep at night.

Negative feedback should be treated as an opportunity to engage and shine by leveraging it to generate discussions that position your company as compassionate and a thought-leader in your industry. Discussions in the public eye almost always are a good thing, as long as you participate in a way that is respectful and logical, and where you've done your best so that both you and the commenter are left in a positive light on the high-road, so to speak.

Enough of the negative, let's move back to the positive. Social media provides free and powerful platforms for direct communication between your customers, prospects, and employees. It is a valuable driver of content distribution and brand visibility online. Years ago, you'd pay thousands of dollars to get the reach that social media provides you today for free. Use this free resource, and leverage it to stay ahead of your competition.

Also from an interview in *Modern Distribution Magazine*, Pamela Kan, President of industrial manufacturer, Bishop-Wisecarver, when asked about their success with and ROI in social media said:

"That's something that we're continuing to refine and get better at. It's definitely great for brand awareness. But for us, it really is a lead-generating machine. The amount of traffic we're able to get to our website or our YouTube channel is outstanding. For a company our size, to have a YouTube channel with more than half a million hits is phenomenal. That's a scale I cannot get through any other advertising medium in our industry. ROI is much easier to track on digital technologies than it is through print. Tell me what you get from doing a print ad; quantify that ROI for me. I can give you much more data around an electronic newsletter than I can over a printed page."

In the same interview, Kan was asked about what she envisioned as the "next big thing" in the social media marketing industry. She replied:

"The Internet with social technologies has truly put the customer in the driver seat. I see manufacturers and distributors who don't believe that this is the reality. And I think some of them are going to pay a really severe price for that. When you have a culture that more and more is telling people that they should be able to have what they want, when they want it, how they want it, to have an industry tell the customer what they can buy, how they can buy it, that's going to be a rude awakening. Ultimately the customer is going to dictate and those companies that create platforms that foster that type of relationship are the ones that are going to win."

While there is a wide array of social networks that your company can use, let's start by focusing on the "big three": Facebook, Twitter, and LinkedIn. It would be remiss of us to not mention to you that Google+ is also becoming a player in the social media space. Google has put a lot of time and money into their social media platform in an effort to compete with the other three, but as of this writing, it's hard to say whether they've gotten it right. The Google+ platform has yet to reach maturity. We've seen Google make some radical changes to Google+ over the past 18 months or so, and we believe it's too early to offer our guidance on it here except to say that your company should build out it's Google+ page, it will be tremendously helpful to your company's SEO efforts, and then take a small bit of time to explore it or, at the very least, keep your eye on it. Google+ isn't as effective as the other three platforms, however, when it comes to engagement.

There are two goals to strive for when it comes to interacting on social media. The first is to get a high volume of comments, and when you do, respond to the comments and engage the readers. The more comments you generate, the larger your audience will grow because friends of friends and connections of connections will see those comments and perhaps jump into the conversation as well. The second is to get a high volume of shares. When you post a valuable piece of content and a reader knows others who would like the content as well, they'll share it. This is also true of videos and images.

When deciding what to share on social media, use a good mix of "edutainment" in your posts to make them more appealing. Remember, without an audience, you won't get clicks, which means the opportunity to generate traffic to your landing pages is drastically reduced. The more likes, favorites, comments and shares you get, the higher our visibility will be in folks' newsfeeds, which increases your opportunity for clicks, traffic and conversion.

Other companies and brands are using social media because it works. Getting more business from social media is no different than any other marketing strategy, and like other marketing strategies, social media will help you to build an audience, drive traffic to your website, and turn that traffic into qualified leads that you will nurture and eventually sell to.

Using Facebook for Business

As of January 2015, Facebook has 1.36 billion active users and is the most popular social network in the world. From a marketing perspective, Facebook serves as a powerful platform for building a community of advocates and increasing word-of-mouth marketing. When deciding whether your distribution company should have a Facebook page, keep in mind that every brand on Facebook is there for one reason – to get more business. Getting more business, however, means different things to different brands and industries. For example, it could mean they are trying to:

- Increase online sales

- Launch a new product

- Build awareness

- Generate leads

By the way, if you spend time wondering whether your ideal clients or prospects spend time on Facebook, here are some statistics from Pew Research Center that may answer that question for you:

- 93% of Facebook users say they are Facebook friends with family members other than parents or children

- 91% say they are Facebook friends with current friends

- 87% say they are connected to friends from the past, such as high school or college classmates

- 58% say they are connected to work colleagues

- 45% say they are Facebook friends with their parents

- 43% say they are friends with their children on Facebook

- 39% say they are connected to people they have never met in person

- 36% say they are Facebook friends with their neighbors

A complaint we often hear is that Facebook can be invasive into your personal life, so consider yourself warned. In order to set up a business page for your company, you must first set up your personal page, and when you set up your personal page, Facebook will ask you a LOT of personal questions including:

- What your hometown is

- Where you went to high school

- Where you went to college

- What your interests are

- Where you work

It will also attempt to raid your personal email address book(s). This is Facebook's attempt at matching you with people from the same town, same schools, same office and whose email address they already have so that you can be "friends". Only share information that you won't mind being publicized, because once you share any information on Facebook, it belongs to them.

When you populate this information, Facebook will find other people with the same alma mater, the same interests or from the same area; and Facebook's algorithms are such that you'll find yourself quickly crossing paths with them. While this is invasive, it's also a great way to find friends on Facebook and build up a base to draw from who you eventually may invite to "like" your company's Facebook page.

Chances are, you already have existing customers and colleagues who would also be more than willing to connect as well, and all of the people you become "friends" with can eventually be invited to like or follow your company's Facebook business page, which is how your social media messages or posts get seen.

In order to grow your Facebook fan base, make your company page on Facebook as discoverable as possible. Don't overlook any opportunity to fully populate every field available on your business's Facebook page. Use a keyword-rich description of your business, including a full overview of what you offer, and the best modes of contacting you. Include a link back to your website along with any other information that will help people understand your business better.

Whether in person, via email, or via Facebook, try asking for as many likes and positive reviews as you are comfortable asking for. On your company page, locate the "Build Audience" menu which will guide you through the process of inviting people to like your page. As mentioned above, uploading a list of email contacts from your email account will enable Facebook to send them each a piece of mail asking them to connect with you. This is not something we'd recommend however. Be conservative in how you promote your page, and respectful of others' time and attention.

Don't "over-promote", especially to uninterested connections. Rather, promote subtly by putting links to each of your social media channels in your email signature and the signatures of your employees with a quick invitation (call-to-action!) to follow or like your company to stay up to date with what's going on. Integrate Facebook into your other online channels. Promote your Facebook presence using the other online and offline marketing channels you already have. Include your Facebook URL on your receipts and all of your communications with vendors and customers. Use Facebook's social plug-ins on your website to get people to engage with your Facebook page while they are visiting your website.

Create a positive experience on your company's Facebook page by sharing great content and interacting with your readers whenever possible. Remember to focus on content that makes your customers' and prospects' jobs easier or their lives better. Stay in tune with your buyer personas so you'll be mindful of what's going to resonate with your audience. If you've written or read a recent blog post or article that would appeal to your prospects, create a sentence or two about a specific point in the article, give your audience an idea of what they'll learn from it, it and share the link. Often when you share a link it will pull an image from the page. If it doesn't, find an image that lends itself well to the subject matter in order to catch the eyes of your readers.

If you are sharing on Facebook about your own blog post or something on your own website, when the link is clicked, you have a chance to collect that lead. Be sure there's a way to opt-in to 'more information' or a special offer. If you are sharing information from a third-party and the link goes back to the third-party's page instead, that's okay. Eventually, you'll have a reputation for sharing great content with no strings attached, positioning yourself as a thought-leader in the industry.

Explore what other distribution companies are doing on their Facebook pages, and see which posts of theirs appear to go unnoticed, and which posts tend to get reactions from readers. Look through your own newsfeed, where you'll discover posts from other companies, and recognize which posts compel you to click or react as well. Ideas for what to share on Facebook to generate leads include typical content that we've already discussed, such as an e-book, a whitepaper, an invitation to an online event, or a blog post, all three of which can lead people back to your landing page. Some indirect sharing that doesn't go back to your page would be images, videos, and third-party content. The key to generating interest on Facebook is to share a variety of content that aligns with your marketing goals while creating value for the reader.

We recommend you consider investing in new likes using Facebook advertising. If you've exhausted all of your existing contacts and need an extra boost in the audience growth department, use Facebook's very powerful demographic targeting capabilities to reach people who are likely to be interested in your business. Facebook offers low-cost, targeted advertising opportunities to either grow your fan base by gaining more likes, or promote your content to those who already have liked the page and may not have seen it. Remember that the people who already have liked your page do not necessarily see your posts.

When done correctly, Facebook will give you great success at reaching your ideal buyer personas to spur your audience growth. In addition to growing likes and getting more exposure to your content, Facebook advertising can drive traffic to your website or drive attendance to an online or live event. A good rule of thumb is to start with a low budget and test the waters when investing in any advertising on social media.

Using Twitter for Business

Twitter is a social network on which, remarkably, people share millions and millions of 140-character messages, and users "follow" or subscribe to each other's updates. As of this writing, Twitter has 284 million active users.

Unless you're a celebrity or your brand is already a household name, amassing a huge following on Twitter isn't exactly a walk in the park. There are, however, a few big levers that can be pulled to more quickly and effectively attract quality followers for your business's Twitter account.

Similar to every other social media profile, optimize your Twitter profile, filling in as much information as possible. Unfortunately, Twitter only provides a fraction of the space other social media platforms give, so let potential followers know who you are, and provide a reason why you're worth a follow as succinctly as possible -- in just two or three sentences at most. Take advantage of the graphical space allotted by choosing a descriptive background, cover image and avatar.

Posts on Twitter are called "Tweets", and the companies that excel on Twitter tweet 24 hours a day, 7 days a week. Tweets appear, to the end user or viewer, in what's called a Twitter feed that cycles continuously, similar to a stock ticker. It doesn't "scroll" like a stock ticker, but new tweets come and old tweets go very quickly with every refresh of your screen. Tweeting every hour or so or even more often is not a bad idea. One of your greatest tactics for growing your followers may even be to tweet around the clock.

People are active on Twitter at different times throughout the day and night, and since interactions on Twitter are so short-lived, the people to engage with may not see your tweets if you don't tweet often enough. To grow your following on Twitter, your company should be visible whenever your prospects and customers are logged in and viewing their feed.

Like Facebook posts, share valuable information to your followers, just a lot more often. To do this definitely requires technology that will automate publishing, scheduling tweets for you throughout the day, and uploading custom images to attract attention to your tweets.

For automated tweeting, one of the most popular tools on the marketplace is HootSuite, another is Buffer. Both of these tools are available at no cost or at low-cost with a few extra bells and whistles built in. There are several more, but for now, these are two of the most highly rated. These tools allow you to automatically schedule and tweet content throughout the day. Tools also allow you to measure the success of each tweet, reporting on things like people "favoriting" the tweet (similar to liking on Facebook, but usually much more exclusive) or "re-tweeting" what you've shared (similar to sharing on Facebook). Both actions will expand the reach of the content you tweet very efficiently.

What could you possibly find to tweet about around the clock? This is where content curation becomes necessary. Because you're tweeting often, it would be ridiculous to expect to create blog posts and white papers all day long, so when it comes to Twitter, tweet information that comes from all sorts of sources including national publications, world news and events, and any other source that is plentiful, entertaining, educational and valuable to your followers and your followers' followers.

There are also many tools available to curate content from. One of the most popular is called Feedly, which is billed as a "one-stop-shop to peruse everything going on in any given industry, allowing you to hand-pick which articles to tweet." Another source of content is Goodreads, and a third we would recommend is Alltop. A fourth tool, LinkedIn Pulse, allows you to follow channels devoted to various industries giving you access to articles featuring top influencers and top news sources.

What would be most powerful to share would be the information that not only is interesting to your followers, but would be interesting to many different groups of people to the point where your followers are recommending or re-tweeting your tweets to their own followers. This eventually would result in the growth of your audience, giving the much-coveted perception of you and/or your company as a thought-leader in the industry.

Another tactic for growing your audience on Twitter is to follow and list people. People get notified via their email and activity feeds when you follow them or list them, and in many cases, when you follow someone, they'll follow you back, growing your audience as a result. It works similarly for creating lists. This is not to say that following people randomly is a good idea. It isn't. Follow people whose opinions and insights you care about and are interested in, and share those tweets to attract like-minded people.

There are several ways to find and follow people you may be interested in. For example, it's possible to find people by importing your email contacts and inviting them to follow you, or by using Twitter's "Who to Follow" tool, located in the "Discover" section of your Twitter account. A fun way to find people to follow is to see who else your followers are following, or who the people you follow are following.

There are public Twitter directories such as Twellow.com, which will give you plenty of ideas. Your Twitter account should be easy to find and follow as well. Include a link to your Twitter account on all of your internet properties, including your website, your blog, and your other social media profiles.

The best tweets are visual. Take the time to include great visuals to add to your tweets. It's been proven again and again that including images pays off in engagement, conversion, and click-through rates. For Twitter, it's best to include an image every three or four tweets. This way, the tweets that do have images tend to stand out from the rest.

You can use Twitter to push out your own tweets and also to monitor the tweets of your customers. Like Facebook, it is a common gathering place where people share about their experiences or search for information. By using hashtags (#) and "at" signs (@), tweets attach to your brand and come up quickly in searches. Using hashtags with your products or during an event you're attending often results in a wave of new followers because people are tuned in to the conversation taking place around that hashtag. Each interaction is public, and serves as a targeted advertisement on your behalf.

It's crucial then that, if your brand has a presence on Twitter, it be monitored. The good news is, this gives you an opportunity to respond immediately to customer inquiries, complaints and praises, all done in the public eye, creating a positive perception of your customer service and of your company, showing it cares what people are saying or needing.

It is worth mentioning that because of the powerful search capability when using hashtags, Twitter is a very powerful platform for sharing products and solutions to people's problems. At one point, Google shared Twitter posts immediately in its search results, and although the agreement between Google and Twitter reached an end a few years later, as of this writing, rumor has it that very soon this will again be the case. This will be extremely helpful when it comes to prospecting for new customers.

Using LinkedIn for Business

LinkedIn was founded in 2003 and is headquartered in Silicon Valley, with offices around the world. It is famous for connecting professionals across the globe. It's got over 330 million members worldwide, including executives from every Fortune 500 company. LinkedIn is the world's largest professional network, and it is also a social network solution used to engage with customers, prospective customers and prospective employees.

It is a truly unique space on the web, one that blurs the lines between a knowledge-sharing platform and a relationship-building tool. Professionals use LinkedIn to search for other professionals, find jobs, advertise, and collaborate in group settings.

Set up a personal LinkedIn page for yourself, and then a LinkedIn company page for your business. Have your employees also set up LinkedIn pages to give your company more exposure. LinkedIn allows you to set up "showcase" pages as well for your products and/or your product lines.

Think of your LinkedIn company page as an online beacon for prospective customers as well as prospective employees. LinkedIn is the first place anyone will look to learn more about your company as well as about you as a professional, so keep both your company page and your personal page up to date, using fresh images the reflect your company's milestones, accomplishments, events and offerings.

Just like with Facebook and Twitter, the first step when starting out with LinkedIn is to make your company easy to find. Your ultimate goal here, too, is to build an engaged audience and to position your business as a thought leader in your industry.

Of course, like the other two platforms we've discussed, optimize your company description on your LinkedIn page using keyword-rich phraseology. Make it easy for the right people to find your company page on LinkedIn by adding keywords in the description and 'Specialties' sections. Similar to the other social media platforms, every like, comment and share will increase your company's reach, so use company page updates to ask questions and engage with your audience. As mentioned earlier, use your company page analytics to test frequency, topics and formats.

Unlike the other two platforms we've discussed, LinkedIn has built in "career" pages that your company can use to attract new talent. These pages give you an opportunity to effectively "speak" directly to candidates who search for positions and find you. According to LinkedIn, "Studies show that a strong employer brand can cut cost-per-hire by over 50%. Use rich media (such as video) on your careers page to showcase yours."

Use LinkedIn's showcase pages to highlight different products, business lines or initiatives in your company with unique messaging and for various audience segments. Keep your showcase pages up to date with news and announcements, share company updates regularly, and allow others to weigh in on your company's activities whenever possible. Every like, comment, and share increases your reach, so prompt your followers to take action on your updates by asking thoughtful questions.

LinkedIn Groups

LinkedIn Groups are probably the most powerful connecting tool in social media today. LinkedIn Groups is an area inside LinkedIn where professionals in similar industries or with similar interests connect, sharing content, finding answers, posting and viewing jobs, making business contacts, and establishing themselves as industry experts. It's the ultimate virtual networking tool for businesspeople. Look for and join various groups or create a group or two. Doing so gives you an opportunity to join in discussions geared toward the distribution industry or any other interest, and get to know other thought-leaders. This will also allow you to position yourself as a thought-leader by managing and participating in these groups, and featuring them on your company page in the featured groups section.

The Art of Social Listening

What may be the most important way to leverage social media for your company's benefit are the industry-related conversations taking place online and recognizing when to respond. Tools we mentioned earlier, like HootSuite, Buffer, as well as a few others can be used to monitor your business and industry mentions in social media, as well as monitor the conversations and social movements of your customers, your hottest prospects, and your competition.

Another tool that has been relatively consistent and reliable is Google Alerts. We recommend you set up multiple Google Alerts for your company, brand, products, leaders, industry terms, and competition. The alerts will get delivered directly to your email inbox at the frequency you indicate (e.g., daily, weekly or as they happen), and they are a great and often (but not always) reliable way to track mentions of your brand and relevant keywords on the web.

CHAPTER 5

CONVERTING VISITORS INTO LEADS

By this point, you understand the importance of optimizing your website, sharing content through blogging, podcasting, videos, and such, and then promoting your content via social media, paid promotion, and other effective channels. If everything is working well together, and you've been consistent and committed to your efforts over a good stretch of time (say, two to three months or so), you're going to start seeing a spike in web traffic.

So what's next? How does all that work and a spike in web traffic translate into new business? People are visiting your website, but are those visits leading to new customers? Or even new leads? The answer will be a resounding no – unless you focus on the real prize... ***Conversion.***

Right now, you are still at the top of your marketing funnel. The next step is to move down the funnel and start converting your website visitors and social media connections into sales leads. To do this, you'll need to come up with a compelling **offer** for your prospects, create a call-to-action to promote that offer, and launch a landing page with a lead capture form for visitors to provide their information in exchange for that offer. Finally, you'll need to measure your results, make any modifications necessary and then repeat and measure the whole process again.

In this section, we will go over the conversion process in more detail. First, let's take a look at the phases of converting visitors into leads, and how this is the best way to turn strangers into customers and promoters of your business:

Phase #1: Create an Offer from Your Content

Your offer, be it an e-book, a video, or some other gated resource, is the most important part of any campaign. It's the initial attraction that catches the attention of your website or social media visitors and gives them a reason to fill out the lead capture form used to collect their information.

Use your offer to target the type of sales leads you're trying to attract. For example, if you're trying to attract golf shops for a new line of golf clubs you're supplying, create offers that will appeal to the buyer personas who you believe could use the new line to improve their business. Perhaps then, your offer would be a white paper of a case study entitled "ABC Golf Shop Shows How Revenue Grew 70% After Introducing New Line of Golf Clubs," or something to that effect.

To ensure you have a solid understanding of the audience you're trying to target with your content offer, don't forget to invest time to develop your buyer personas. We discussed this in Chapter 1, but as a reminder, a buyer persona is a semi-fictional representation of your ideal customer, which is based on actual customer data.

So again, if you were a sporting goods distributor with a new putter you're trying to promote, you might have a buyer persona named "Gary Golf Store Owner." And through a combination of research, surveys, and interviews, you know that Gary is in his mid-40s, he plays golf twice a week himself, he carries all the golf accessories and gadgets in his store, and he prefers watching product videos vs. reading catalogs. Armed with this kind of detailed information, you'll have a great starting point for creating a targeted content offer. Just remember to target your offer toward what you know Gary will find valuable. It's not about tooting your own horn; rather it's about supporting your customers' (Gary's) needs.

In addition to content-focused offers, product-focused offers can include a custom consultation, free trial, or demo of your product. Of course, there's no reason to be constrained by what's typical. Use anything you think will work for your target customers. Also, keep in mind that the offer is a conversation starter for the sales team, so it should be designed to start a conversation that will lead to a sale.

Phase #2: Create Irresistible Calls-to-Action (CTAs)

Once you decide on your offer, create a few compelling calls-to-action (CTAs) to go with it. As we mentioned earlier, a call-to-action is an image or a link of text that grabs a visitor's attention and directs that visitor to take action, usually driving them to a landing page. Calls-to-action link your readers to the next step that will engage them further with your company.

Calls-to-action are located everywhere: on website pages, in emails and blog posts, throughout your social media, within content offers, etc. **They are the key trigger behind lead generation.**

The action you invite people to take could be anything from downloading an e-book, tweeting out or posting a message on social media, signing up for a webinar, downloading a coupon, signing up for an event, and so on.

Calls-to-action should be used in every piece of your marketing, including press releases, social media posts, and at trade shows, in addition to what's already been mentioned previously. A good rule of thumb to follow when preparing each piece of marketing you turn out is to ask yourself "What do I want people to do after they see this piece?" Even when posting to social media, think about what step you'd like your reader to take after he or she reads it. Doing so will give you more clarity as to what to include in your call-to-action.

The more effective a call-to-action is, the greater your lead generation will be, so take the time to understand the various components of a call-to-action. There are several crucial elements to include that will entice people to take an action based on your content, so we'll talk a bit about them here.

Remember that a call-to-action shouldn't always be to purchase your product or service. While you'd like to lead them in that direction, leads need to be nurtured, and so guide your reader gently through the process of getting to know your company better first.

For example, a social media post may include a call-to-action instructing the reader to check out your blog, with a link to your blog. Then, a call-to-action in your blog post might offer that the reader download an e-book. Somewhere inside that e-book, there may then be a call-to-action to obtain a trial offer of your product or service. Although these calls-to-action are leading the prospect in the right direction, there is still no direct selling going on.

The key components of a quality call-to-action are:

- Copy that makes people take action

- An eye-catching design

- A clear value proposition

- A landing page that aligns with an appropriate state in the sales cycle

Here are some quick tips about writing an effective call-to-action:

Include a Subject and a Verb. Often the subject of a call-to-action is an "understood you", where the verb tells the reader (i.e., "you") to do something (click here, check this out, read this, visit our website, download an e-book, etc.) A good rule of thumb to follow is 1) tell the reader exactly what to do, and 2) try to keep it to only one call-to-action per message. If given the choice between two options, statistics show most readers will choose neither. If it's absolutely necessary to have two calls-to-action, keep them separate enough on the web page so that they don't compete with each other.

Use Numbers. Including numbers in your calls-to-action will greatly improve your conversions. Numbers grab attention and help to clarify questions in the heads of your readers, removing any ambiguity. Using numbers has proven effective not only in calls-to-action, but also in blog post titles, press release headlines, and email subject lines. For example, instead of offering a white paper, offer a 25-page white paper. Instead of offering a discount, offer a 15% discount. Instead of offering a video, offer a 10-minute video. Believe it or not, this subtle tweak will make a big difference.

Personalize with "Smart" CTAs. HubSpot's Jeff Russo conducted an analysis of over 93,000 calls-to-action from their database of customers. He found that personalized calls-to-action that targeted the user had a 42% higher view-to-submission rate than calls-to-action that were the same for all visitors. Personalization is done through a technology that allows you to provide the right call-to-action to visitors of your website based on their behavior during previous visits and where they are in your sales cycle. It's incredibly effective.

Keep it Concise. Never write copy that takes a reader a long time to read. Keep it short and simple. The same rule holds true for all of your marketing. You have a limited opportunity to capture and hold a visitor's attention, so get them to take action before they're on to something else, like a competitor's website. Write only as much as necessary to make your point, and once your point is made, stop.

Be Creative. Let's face it -- CTAs that use words like 'click here' or 'submit' or 'get' are boring. Instead, consider kicking it up a notch by using verbs that are more vibrant and interesting, and that even subtly suggest benefits to the reader, such as 'browse', 'compare', 'jump', or 'grab'. Also, consider using interactivity on your call-to-action buttons by using hover effects that cause the CTA to change when the cursor hovers over it. Create buttons that change color and brightness, take on a shadow effect, and change size all to better entice that coveted click. The button should look like it's clickable by using shadow effects to create some depth.

Keep it Above the Fold. Place your call-to-action "above the fold", that is, at the top section of the web page it's placed on. Don't count on the readers to scroll down the page – there's a good chance they won't. Both the upper left area and the upper right area of a website are normally the most successful in grabbing readers' attention; however, this is something that should be tested because success is also dependent on the placement of other content on your web page as well.

Phase #3: Create Landing Pages That Convert

The landing page is where your website visitors arrive after they click on your call-to-action, and where they will fill out the form to download your offer.

This is where excellent writing skills matter most. Being able to articulate ideas clearly will help capture the attention of the visitors who come to your landing pages. This is crucial. Visitors focus on the words on the page more than on the graphics, so in order to ensure the copy is compelling enough to get the visitor to opt in, be sure it's as clear and persuasive as possible. Graphics will help convey meaning and strengthen the message, but if the copy doesn't draw visitors in, they'll leave, and your lead is gone.

Clearly emphasize the benefits of your offer. Describe how the piece of content the reader is considering will make their lives or their companies better in some way. Stay away from technical jargon, as it tends to add complexity. Once visitors submit their information on a landing page, they should be redirected to a thank-you page where they can access the offer.

Your sales team will then use the information you ask for in the form to follow up ... provided it's a quality lead, which you can gauge by using lead scoring. Lead scoring ties back to personalization. It's a method used by tracking a lead's behaviors and activity on your website, giving you an idea of their level of interest as well as insight as to whether they fit one of your buyer personas. Combining both factors enables you to have a better determination of the quality of the lead.

Phase #4: Testing, Measuring, Repeating

Content offers, calls-to-action, and landing pages are the core elements of the conversion process, but let's not stop there. If you only have one single conversion pathway, you'll have very little insight into the process and the way it performs. In order to improve your conversion process, measure and experiment continuously.

Marketing metrics to watch include the click-through rate of your call-to-action, the conversion rate of your landing page, and the number of new leads and sales an offer generates.

In order to determine which elements best help you achieve your goals, test different CTAs, landing pages, and offers. If a call-to-action has been on your home page for a month, vary the messaging or swap out an entirely new CTA, and after another month, measure which one performed best.

If landing page conversions are low, make a change to the page layout and measure the results. Don't be afraid to test different variations; it's easy to switch back if the old version worked better. It will be worth it to run split A/B tests and discover the best combination of words, colors, graphics and calls-to-action that increase your website's conversions. Most landing page and lead capture software has split-testing built right into it, making this easy to do. Remember to run only one A/B test at a time, changing one variable each time in order to better identify which element(s) of your sales funnel triggered each of the results your are seeing.

Phase #5: Nurture Your Leads Into Customers

Lead nurturing is the process of developing relationships with your potential customers by sending targeted, relevant, and valuable messages to them in a timely manner. We'll talk more about this in the next chapter on email marketing. Remember that your marketing is an integrated system that combines different channels and assets. Social media and blogging might do wonders with attracting traffic to your website, but lead generation tools should also be in place not only to capture that traffic, but also to automatically market to the leads you capture, nurturing them through the sales funnel.

The end goal is to get your leads to "raise their hand" and self-select into further engaging with your business. From a technical standpoint, a lead nurturing system is software that allows you to send an automated series of email messages to early-stage leads in order to pre-qualify them before handing them over to your sales team. Getting leads is very exciting -- but when first captured, leads are rarely at the point where they can be considered sales-ready.

Do you have an existing sales funnel? If so, how long does it typically take for a lead to become a customer after his or her first inquiry? Does the sales cycle vary for different types of purchases? Equipped with the answers to these questions, you're ready to build some effective lead nurturing campaigns and leverage your marketing channels to better qualify leads and help your sales organization.

A key variable to a successful marketing campaign is the degree to which the sales funnel is targeted. If a sales process or funnel is well-targeted, you may generate fewer leads, but you'll have a much higher conversion rate and a greater chance for a sale. For this reason, create marketing funnels for every buyer persona who qualifies as an ideal customer for your business. Take into consideration such things as targeting the industries that are the most profitable, the demographics of the average buyer, their common interests and styles, and the job functions of the decision-makers.

CHAPTER 6

EMAIL MARKETING

In addition to nurturing your leads using targeted email messages, let's take a look at and work towards the larger email marketing picture, growing your list or database, closely following key metrics, and increasing conversions. This is often done successfully through a well-written email marketing campaign that, with each email, brings a prospect closer to a sale.

Email is an efficient and cost-effective tool that enables you to reach a large audience, but it carries with it some pretty strict guidelines. Rule number one is, of course, to never spam. Spamming is a catch-all phrase for improper use of an email system whether it be mailing too often, mailing non-valuable, annoying or "salesy" information, or mailing without permission. No one enjoys receiving spam, so be respectful and careful about what you send to your audiences or you may find yourself unsubscribed to and even reported for using spammy tactics.

Despite what you may have read in the past, email remains one of the most effective methods of marketing today, especially now that smartphones and tablets have become so popular. Email is instant, and people have easy access to their email accounts, so what doesn't get opened on your recipients' desktop at work, has an excellent chance of being opened on their smartphone or tablet during off-hours. Before smartphones took over our lives, this wasn't the case.

Email marketing tools continue to evolve at a rapid pace. Using a combination of a good CRM and a robust email marketing tool, you have the ability to segment your email lists, tagging or making notations on each list member to help you better track and understand their behaviors. This process helps you better refine your targeting efforts and tailor your emails toward individual audiences.

It also gives you the ability to track whether an individual opened your mail, how many times they opened it, and how much time they spent reading it. The analytics these tools provide show you which recipients were interested in which pieces of content you shared by using measureable text links that you include in your email. Again, technology today enables you to track all of your marketing efforts, and learn which marketing tactics work and are worth investing more time and effort into, and which strategies or tactics do not generate interest from your targeted audience.

List Building

Once you have a visitor to your landing page or even your website's home page, or your social media page, your primary goal is to give them a reason to opt-in to join your mailing list. Visitors to your website or landing page know that if they opt-in to what you're offering, in all likelihood, they'll receive future emails from you. The idea is to get them interested in what you're offering, and to also be willing to receive future emails from you. This will be one of your biggest marketing challenges -- creating opt-in opportunities and penning emails that appeal to an audience.

When writing the copy on your landing page as well as the email sequences that follow, ask yourself: What's so valuable about your emails? What interesting and unique information will they receive in your email newsletter? Be explicit and phrase the benefits in a way your audience will understand.

Only send messages to people who have explicitly opted in. Follow the extreme principle of Seth Godin's "permission marketing": would your recipient be upset if they didn't receive your message? If yes, go ahead and send your email.

Send emails only that are relevant to the interests of your contacts. Talk to them and share with them. Don't talk at them or be "salesy". Keep in mind what initially brought them to you. How can you follow-up on that interest to further engage them? Be as personal as professionally acceptable in your communication. Use a real email sender name, and use a personalized signature. Personalize the message as well so the recipient remembers how and why they came to your website. For example, start with "you recently checked out our e-book..." or "thanks for subscribing to our blog."

When deciding what to write about, your message should always give value to the reader. Get into the minds of your recipients and answer the question they are wondering about as they decide whether to open and read your mail, which is "What's in it for me?" Are you emailing them to tell them how great your product is? Or are you offering to help them solve a problem? Make the value clear in both the email body and especially in subject line.

Be predictable and known for the quality of your emails, so that readers continue to open and read them. Time them out tastefully, and balance any perception of a sales message with the over-delivery of value first. Use your email messages to position yourself as the industry expert, which can only be done if you're gaining the respect of your reader by providing valuable and much-needed advice to them.

Using images in your email is great for engagement, but don't rely on images, as some email clients don't load images automatically, and some recipients choose not to have the images displayed. If your email is one large image, your recipient might not have any idea what it's about. Instead, use images as accompanying content in your email along with text links, and include enough text without the image to communicate value in case the image doesn't appear.

Most people wonder how often they should send email, or what to do with a list or database that they haven't mailed to in a long time. Be consistent in your communication to set the right expectations in recipients. Whether you send your messages daily, weekly, or monthly, pick a schedule and stick to it. If it's been 6 months to a year since you've last emailed, chances are, your email list will be a bit stale, so expect some bounce backs. In this case, a brief introduction at the beginning of your email may be a good idea to re-engage your audience. Start off with a note stating where you've been or why it's been so long. Keep it light and engaging, and have a good reason for writing them out of the blue after so much time has passed.

Each one of your marketing messages should have a goal. Make it clear what recipients are supposed to do once they open your email. Are you driving subscribers to read a product announcement on your blog? Or perhaps you are asking them to share an offer on social media or inviting them to download your new e-book. Whatever it is you'd like your reader to do, be as clear as possible, and ask them to do only one thing per message. As we mentioned earlier, most people, when given a choice between two options, will choose neither one.

If your goal is to segment or better-target your list, include a call-to-action that links to a landing page on which the recipient can reconvert and self-select to further engage with your company. Although these subscribers are already existing leads for your business, this will inform them about product-specific offers and allow them to qualify themselves as more sales-ready. If they are not ready to commit yet, continue nurturing them with broader offers, keeping your company top of mind for them.

Remember, the landing page is part of your email campaign. Email marketing doesn't stop with a click. Your landing page is an extension of your email, and it is where your conversion takes place. Your email offer and landing page should be aligned, using similar messaging, language or tone, and colors and images.

Measuring Email Performance

Your email campaign's click-through rate (CTR) is used to measure response. This is the metric that tells us how many of your recipients clicked on your link(s). The CTR can give you a sense of how compelling your offer and email messages are. Experiment with different offers, subject lines, calls-to-action, and timing to improve your email CTR. Why do we measure the CTR vs. the open rate? The open rate can be an unreliable metric. The open rate is tracked by a tiny image embedded in your email, and several major email clients fail to load that image. As such, the open rate metric you generate will often be inaccurate. Instead of worrying about open rate, therefore, focus on the number of clicks your emails receive.

The unsubscribe rate measures the percentage of recipients who opted out of or chose to stop receiving your email communications. As with open rates, the unsubscribe rate isn't a reliable picture of your email list's health either. Don't let the unsubscribes get you down. People opt out for many reasons, not only because they are no longer interested. On the other hand, many subscribers won't bother to go through the formal unsubscribe process but will simply stop opening, reading, and clicking on your messages.

Measure how many of your click-throughs turned into reconversions on your landing page. This is the ultimate measure of an email campaign's effectiveness. The higher your conversion rate, the more relevant and compelling the offer was for your audience. However, conversion rates are dependent on factors beyond the original email message, such as the quality of your landing page. Always test different landing pages with your emails to improve your reconversion rate.

CHAPTER 7

WHAT TO MEASURE, HOW TO SUCCEED

We covered how to use lead nurturing and email marketing to follow up with your leads and engage them an on ongoing basis to lead them through the sales funnel. However, nurturing your contacts doesn't have to be limited to email communications. Consider behavior-driven communications as well; these are the communications that get triggered based on your leads' full history of interactions, both on and off your website.

As you examine further down toward your sales and marketing funnel, review the performance of your various marketing activities, identify the activities that give you the best results, and eliminate or modify the ineffective campaigns. Here are some metrics to monitor and suggestions for continuing to refine your internet marketing strategy.

When you review your marketing activities and making decisions about which areas to focus on, figure out what needs to improve and then take the appropriate steps.

- Do you need more traffic to your blog?

- Are enough visitors to your website converting into leads?

Get into the mindset of constantly looking for new opportunities and set metrics for success. In almost all cases, your metrics should be quantifiable and involve a set time frame. For example, "Increase website leads by X% over the next X days."

Analyze how each of your programs perform, and make changes with the intention of achieving your marketing goals by doing less of what doesn't work and more what works. Modify what doesn't work so that it works better.

In order for your refinements to have a big impact, monitor several key factors. Therefore, before diving into how to improve them, let's first discuss what the relevant metrics are.

Traffic: Overall, how many people are coming to your website? Look into what channel drove the most and least visits. Take that knowledge, make iterations and launch campaigns that will increase visits.

Leads: How much of this traffic are you converting into leads and potential customers? This number should be constantly growing to ensure a steady flow of revenue.

Customers: Always be measuring your campaigns and channels toward customer acquisition. How many sales did you close this month? How does that compare to last month's performance? The ability to make this comparison is invaluable.

Customer Acquisition Cost: How much are you investing to draw in each new customer? If you rely primarily on outbound marketing methods, like trade shows and direct mail, your cost per customer is probably pretty high. If you are following the steps outlined in this book and focus on inbound marketing, in all likelihood, you are saving your company a lot of money.

New vs. Repeat Traffic: Of your overall traffic, how many visitors are returning to your website, and how many new people are finding you? Both types of visitors are good. Attracting new visitors means people are finding you through search. Attracting repeat visitors means you've given people good reason to come back to your website. The key is finding a balance.

Effectiveness by Channel: What promotion channels or referring sources are sending you the most traffic? Focus on long-term results, not short-term traffic spurts you might get from news coverage or press releases.

Continue to measure based on a decided timeframe, and determine if you've met your metrics or goals successfully. If so, stick with what you're doing. If not, see what you could have done differently, and focus on the improvements that give you the best long-term results.

Taking Steps for Improvement

There are several areas to review when you're not getting the results you desire or expect. Failing metrics could be due to any of the following issues, or even a combination of them. Adjust each issue and measure the results in order to isolate the problem to the best of your ability.

Keywords: Try new keywords or variations of keywords to see if they help you get found more often. Since each page on your website can incorporate different keywords, this is quite easy to do.

Search Engine Optimization (SEO): See if changing a simple on-page SEO factor can help boost visits. Examples of on-page factors are page title, meta description, and headings. As a simple test, try changing the page title of one of your key web pages to see if you generate more traffic.

Conversion Tactics: Try new things with your conversion forms or landing pages. For example, make a change to the layout by moving the form's placement on the web page or use an image that's completely different from what you currently have. Try different colors and different fonts, different images and different calls-to-action. It's been tested and proven that making changes to all of these things will contribute greatly to conversion results.

Content: Determine which content is bringing you the most traffic and leads. This could be an opportunity to either focus more on that kind of content, or refine your promotion of other content pieces or modes.

Social Media: Evaluate which social media channels are generating the most website visitors and leads. Again, either focus on your successful social media platforms, or try improving your performance in your less successful channels.

Lead Nurturing and Email Marketing: - Maybe you're sending emails too frequently -- or not frequently enough. Maybe the calls-to-action in your email are not appropriate for your audience. Keep experimenting and testing.

Internet marketing might seem difficult, overwhelming or daunting, but by tackling each internet marketing tactic step by step, it becomes more manageable and produces results. Believe us when we tell you... You CAN do this!

We hope that by reading this book, you've gained a better understanding of which internet marketing essentials will improve your wholesale distribution business's overall marketing program and help you achieve business growth.

ABOUT THE AUTHORS

Susan M. Merlo, President
Next Level iMedia Marketing

Susan Merlo is a well-known marketing strategist, trainer, speaker and best-selling author and has created several successful businesses after having worked 20 years in a corporate environment. She is the CEO and Founder of Next Level iMedia, a smart and savvy marketing firm headquartered in New Fairfield, Connecticut.

She specializes in both on-line and off-line marketing, and generates an unprecedented amount of exposure for her clients by implementing effective lead generation and follow up strategies that result in a steady stream of leads, and demonstrating significant growth in both new and repeat sales.

To learn more about Susan visit www.SusanMerlo.com.

Jon C. Dupree, President
Calibrate Marketing & Mentoring

Jon Dupree is the owner of Calibrate Marketing & Mentoring with over two decades of experience positioning products and companies in the B2B market. His intimate knowledge of how sales and marketing co-exist has resulted in a unique perspective for communicating with the online community. He has successfully trained and developed marketing strategies for start-ups and small to mid-sized businesses to improve their digital performance for e-mail, search and social media. Jon integrates the insight from marketing and customer data to continually obtain greater response and ROI from these strategies. Jon holds an Economics degree from Syracuse University and has been certified as an ISO 9000 auditor.

Made in the USA
San Bernardino, CA
26 February 2015